MILITARY AIRCRAFT
B-2 SPIRIT STEALTH BOMBER

BY JOHN HAMILTON

VISIT US AT
WWW.ABDOPUBLISHING.COM

Published by ABDO Publishing Company, PO Box 398166, Minneapolis, MN 55439.
Copyright ©2012 by Abdo Consulting Group, Inc. International copyrights reserved in all
countries. No part of this book may be reproduced in any form without written permission
from the publisher. A&D Xtreme™ is a trademark and logo of ABDO Publishing Company.

Printed in the United States of America, North Mankato, Minnesota.
102011
012012

 PRINTED ON RECYCLED PAPER

Editor: Sue Hamilton
Graphic Design: Sue Hamilton
Cover Design: John Hamilton
Cover Photo: U.S. Air Force
Interior Photos: All photos United States Air Force except: Department of Defense-pgs
14-15, 25 & 28-29; and Northrop Grumman-pg 26 (inset).

ABDO Booklinks
Web sites about Military Aircraft are featured on our Book Links pages. These links are
routinely monitored and updated to provide the most current information available. Web
site: www.abdopublishing.com

Library of Congress Cataloging-in-Publication Data

Hamilton, John, 1959-
  B-2 Spirit stealth bomber / John Hamilton.
     p. cm. -- (Xtreme military aircraft)
  Includes index.
  ISBN 978-1-61783-267-3
  1. B-2 bomber--Juvenile literature. I. Title.
  UG1242.B6H339 2012
  623.74'63--dc23
                          2011042342

TABLE OF CONTENTS

B-2 SPIRIT ☆
STEALTH ☆
BOMBER ☆

The B-2 Spirit is a
United States Air Force
multi-role heavy bomber.
It is one of America's
deadliest weapons. Its
stealth technology makes it
almost invisible to radar. The B-2
can fly undetected thousands of
miles deep into enemy territory.

XTREME
FACT

The B-2 Spirit stealth bomber has a
wingspan about half the length of a
football field, but on a radar screen it
looks as small as a bird.

MISSION

The B-2 Spirit is designed to fly undetected deep into enemy territory. Its stealth design allows it to penetrate heavy anti-aircraft defenses. Because of this special ability, the B-2 is used to destroy high-value targets such as radar installations, airfields, or anti-aircraft missile sites.

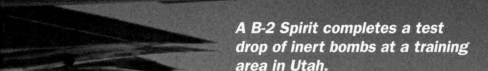

A B-2 Spirit completes a test drop of inert bombs at a training area in Utah.

XTREME FACT

The B-2 Spirit stealth bomber can drop up to eighty 500-pound (230-kg) GPS-guided bombs or sixteen 2,400-pound (1,100-kg) nuclear bombs.

ORIGINS

The B-2 program was started in the late 1970s. The bombers were designed to carry nuclear weapons undetected into the Soviet Union in the event of war. But in the 1980s, the Cold War ended with the breakup of the Soviet Union. The B-2's role changed. Instead of nuclear weapons, it now carries regular gravity bombs or precision-guided "smart" bombs.

The first B-2, named Spirit of Missouri, *was delivered to the United States Air Force in 1993. In total, 21 bombers have been manufactured. Twenty are still in active service today.*

B-2 Spirit stealth bombers have a total program cost of about $2.1 billion per aircraft. That includes research and development costs.

CREW

B-2 Spirit bombers each have two crew members. The pilot sits on the left side of the cockpit, while the mission commander sits on the right. In comparison, a B-52 bomber requires a crew of five.

The B-2 cockpit includes electronic flight instruments that give the crew information about the flight, the engines, weapons status, and enemy targets.

B-2 Spirit pilots are Air Force officers with college degrees and extensive flying experience. Competition to become a B-2 pilot is intense.

B-2 SPIRIT STEALTH BOMBER FAST FACTS

B-2 Spirit Stealth Bomber Specifications

Function:	Multi-role heavy bomber
Service Branch:	U.S. Air Force
Manufacturer:	Northrop Grumman Corp.
Crew:	2
Length:	69 feet (21 m)
Height:	17 feet (5 m)
Wingspan:	172 feet (52 m)
Maximum Takeoff Weight:	336,500 pounds (152,634 kg)
Maximum Airspeed:	Mach 0.95 (550 knots, 633 mph, 1,019 kph)
Ceiling:	50,000-plus feet (15,240 m)
Combat Range:	6,000 nautical miles (6,905 miles, or 11,113 km)

STEALTH

The B-2 Spirit is often called a stealth bomber.
Its shape has few sharp edges, making it almost
invisible to enemy radar.

Instead of aluminum, B-2s are made of carbon-fiber composite materials, with a special coating that absorbs radar.

A technician checks out a B-2 Spirit bomber at Nellis Air Force Base in Las Vegas, Nevada.

FLYING WING

B-2 Spirits use a "flying wing" style of construction. This shape is very difficult to detect on radar. It is also aerodynamically unstable.

To keep B-2s stable, sophisticated sensors and computers automatically make adjustments to the aircrafts' steering. Without this high-tech assistance, it would be almost impossible for B-2 pilots to safely fly the planes.

The B-2 Spirit is a leap in bomber technology, capable of bringing massive firepower to places that were previously unreachable.

ENGINES

The B-2 is powered
by four General
Electric F118-GE-100
turbofan engines. They are
mounted in the body of the wing
just behind and to the sides of the
cockpit. This reduces their infrared (heat)
signature, making them harder to detect by
enemy forces. These powerful engines help the
B-2 fly at just below Mach 1, the speed of sound.

B-2 Spirits use a system that injects special chemicals into the engine exhaust, which reduces the telltale white contrail that jets leave behind as they fly.

An Air Force staff sergeant inspects an engine intake of a B-2.

RESCUE

RANGE

Because of its aerodynamic shape and use of lightweight carbon-fiber composites in its construction, the B-2 Spirit bomber can fly about 6,000 miles (9,656 km) without refueling. With mid-air refueling, the B-2's range is almost unlimited. Some B-2 missions have lasted more than 30 hours in the air.

A KC-10A Extender aerial tanker from McGuire Air Force Base, New Jersey, refuels a B-2 Spirit during a training exercise.

WEAPONS

Each B-2 Spirit can carry up to 40,000 pounds (18,144 kg) of bombs, either conventional or nuclear, in two weapons bays in the center of the plane. The weapons can be regular gravity bombs or precision-guided bombs, which use lasers, infrared, or GPS coordinates to guide them to their targets.

Air Force weapons specialists prepare to load a BDU-56 practice bomb onto a B-2 Spirit.

The plane's bomb racks can hold up to 80 500-pound (227-kg) conventional bombs, or 16 nuclear weapons. B-2s can also launch AGM-158 cruise missiles. These advanced stealth weapons can attack well-defended land targets. They have a range of about 575 miles (925 km), further increasing the lethal punch of the B-2 bomber.

BASES

B-2 Spirit of Alaska sits in its hanger at Whiteman AFB ready to leave for a combat mission in Iraq.

Nineteen of the Air Force's fleet of 20 B-2 Spirit bombers are based at Whiteman Air Force Base, Missouri, home of the 509th Bomb Wing. Specially constructed hangers with strict climate control keep the B-2s' stealth materials in top condition.

XTREME FACT

Because of the B-2s' long combat range, they can take off from Whiteman AFB, carry out their mission in far-away combat zones such as the Middle East, and then return safely to base. Some missions last more than 30 hours.

B-2s are sometimes based in three other locations: Andersen Air Force Base on the Pacific Ocean island of Guam (shown here); RAF Fairford standby airfield in England; and the island of Diego Garcia in the Indian Ocean.

COMBAT HISTORY

A B-2 Spirit bomber flies through the clouds during a training flight.

B-2 Spirit bombers have been used in combat since 1999.

B-2 Spirit bombers were first used in combat in the Kosovo War in 1999. They used satellite-guided bombs to destroy enemy targets. B-2s have also flown in combat missions in Afghanistan, Iraq, and Libya.

THE FUTURE

The U.S. Air Force plans to use the B-2 Spirit bomber for many years to come. Eventually, the B-2 will need to be upgraded or replaced. Already, Air Force planners are working on a new generation of "mini-B-2s," which will be more advanced yet cheaper to make. They may also be unmanned, like current Predator drones.

The Air Force hopes to have this new generation of long-range bombers ready to fly by the mid-2020s. It may also rely on the new F-35 Lightning II fighter to carry out some of the B-2's current missions. In the meantime, the stealthy, deadly B-2 Spirit remains a crucial weapon in America's arsenal.

An Air Force senior airman guards the entry point to a B-2 Spirit bomber at Andersen Air Force Base in Guam.

29

GLOSSARY

COLD WAR

The Cold War was a time of political, economic, and cultural tension between the United States and its allies and the Soviet Union and other Communist nations. It lasted from about 1947, just after the end of World War II, until the early 1990s, when the Soviet Union collapsed and Communism was no longer a major threat to the United States.

CONTRAIL

Condensed water from an aircraft's engines that is trailed behind when flying at high altitude. Contrails look like white streaks against the sky.

INFRARED

Part of the electromagnetic spectrum that has wavelengths that are too long to be part of visible light. Infrared light includes thermal radiation, or heat.

Kosovo War
A war fought between the southeastern European nations of Kosovo and Yugoslavia in 1998-1999. In 1999, NATO countries, including the United States, helped Kosovo in its war for independence.

Mach
A common way to measure the speed of an aircraft when it approaches or exceeds the speed of sound in air. An aircraft traveling at Mach 1 is moving at the speed of sound, about 768 miles per hour (1,236 kph) when the air temperature is 68 degrees Fahrenheit (20 degrees C). An aircraft traveling at Mach 2 would be moving at twice the speed of sound.

Precision-Guided Weapons
Precision-guided weapons, also called "smart bombs," are bombs or missiles that can be steered in mid-air toward their targets. The B-2 Spirit can launch several kinds of precision-guided weapons, or "munitions." These include bombs and missiles that are guided by lasers, radar, or satellite signals.

Radar
A way to detect objects, such as aircraft or ships, using electromagnetic (radio) waves. Radar waves are sent out by large dishes, or antennas, and then strike an object. The radar dish then detects the reflected waves, which can tell operators how big an object is, how fast it is moving, its altitude, and its direction. B-2 Spirit bombers use modern stealth construction to minimize their radar reflection, making them very difficult for enemy forces to detect.

INDEX